Coaching and Mentoring

The Salt and Pepper for Employee
Potential Development.

Copyright Notice

Contents

Preface

You are in your office looking over your performance report and it happened again. Your low performing employee failed to meet quota this month even after you spoke with them about the importance of meeting goals. This employee has a great attitude and you know they can do better. You just do not know how to motivate them to reach the goal. Money used to work, but that has worn off. You are baffled and you know being frustrated makes matters worse. What do you do?

This Coaching and Mentoring book focuses on how to better coach your employees to higher performance. Coaching is a process of relationship building and setting goals. How well you coach is related directly to how well you are able to foster a great working relationship with your employees through understanding them and strategic goal setting.

Whilst Coaching and Mentoring are very different, balanced correctly they are to employee potential development what correctly added salt and pepper are to good food.

Chapter One:
Defining Coaching and Mentoring

We are all capable of change and growth; we just need to know where to begin.
-Blaine Lee

Before getting deep into the subject of coaching, it is prudent to discuss mentoring and what it tries to achieve. Understanding the difference between coaching and mentoring will help you be clear on your coaching objective. Many times, these two concepts are misunderstood.

The goal of this chapter is to define both concepts and introduce a coaching model that will allow you to focus on improving performance. Let us begin by defining what coaching is.

WHAT IS COACHING?

A coach tutors or instructs a person to achieve a specific goal or skill. In baseball, a batting coach only focuses on the mechanics of hitting the ball. They spend time instructing the hitter how to change their swing to improve their performance. They give exercises and goals to the hitter that target the swing of the bat.

In the office environment, you may see similar coaches helping others improve a skill. They may be sales coaches or customer service coaches. No matter what the area of focus is, a coach specializes on improving one or two areas of development at a time.

Here are some characteristics of a coach:

- Trainer
- Instructor
- Tutor
- Focus on one or two skills at a time
- Their interaction is planned and structured

WHAT IS MENTORING?

Mentoring has a different purpose and goal. Mentoring is the act of guiding, counseling, and supporting. This is vastly different from coaching. It is fundamentally teaching. However, the objective is slightly different.

Mentorship is more voluntary in nature and is less formal than coaching. The mentor and protégé endeavor on a broad development goal like becoming a leader. Mentoring encompasses many complex areas of development.

In your matching activity, we learned that coaching scenarios include the following:

- Sales
- Customer service
- Production work
- Behavioral issues like tardiness

Likewise, we learned that mentoring scenarios include the following:

- Networking
- Political strategizing

- Negotiation
- Managing

In this book, you will learn how to effectively coach; however, later, there will be a discussion on how to transition from a coach to a mentor. It should be a manager's goal to develop their people in a way that furthers their career. Mentoring does this. For now, we are going to focus on coaching people for specific goals. The next lesson discusses an easy-to-remember coaching process.

INTRODUCING THE G.R.O.W. MODEL

Having a consistent and uniform approach to coaching enables you to coach more effectively with strategy and direction. Using a coaching model will also instill confidence in your employee, because they see a methodical approach. When we approach coaching haphazardly, we become disorganized and this creates frustrating coaching sessions.

The GROW model helps you organize your coaching process in a flow that identifies the goal first and ends with putting a plan together. Here are the details of the GROW model:

- **Goal setting**: a goal has to be set in order to give direction and purpose to the coaching session. Ambiguous goals are usually never achieved. Setting the goal first shapes your discussion with your employee and sets the tone.

- **Reality check**: both you and your employee must come to terms on the current state or level of performance or any issues that are causing breakdowns. Getting to the bottom of the problem begins with identifying and claiming it. From there obstacles are better identified.

- **Options developed**: here you and your employee explore action steps that will help them improve their performance. Usually goals or options that are prefabricated by an employee's manager result in poor buy-in and missed goals. Allow your employee to explore options they develop.

- **Wrap it up with a plan**: once you nail down an option or two, it is time to strike it down on paper so to speak. If it is not written down, it won't happen. Creating a well-defined plan is essential in order to know the direction you need to go and to demonstrate success or failure.

GROW is simple yet powerful. Following the GROW process consistently will develop a natural process for you. Coaching should be natural. This puts you and your employee at ease, making the process more valuable and rewarding. Let us unpack the GROW model over the next few chapters and see how to incorporate it into our daily work lives.

PRACTICAL ILLUSTRATION

Sharon was assigned to coach a new employee named Brad who worked in the sales department. Brad had been promising as an applicant, yet his sales did not live up to expectations. Sharon decided to have a meeting to determine the problem and create a plan to resolve it. First they decided upon a goal, which was to boost his sales. Sharon found out from Brad that customers had a hard time understanding him through his accent, so they looked at their options. After weighing the choices, Brad decided to attend a speech class. They created a plan that outlined what his expected sales would be and how they correlate to his progress in speech class. Brad eventually was able to reach those expectations, and Sharon had successfully coached him.

Chapter Two:
Setting Goals

*If you don't know where you are going, you will
probably end up somewhere else.*
Lawrence J. Peter

Without a goal, your chances of successfully coaching your
employee to better performance are low. Defining specific,
measureable, attainable, realistic, and time driven goals will
plot a marker in the horizon that acts as your beacon. Without
it, you are navigating blindly, causing frustration for both you
and your employee, because you never seem to make any
improvement. It becomes a constant cycle of failing to meet the
goal and talking to your employee about it. This repeats
continually without a well-defined goal.

This chapter will discuss setting **goals** with an easy-to-
remember technique. This is the first component or the "G" of
the **GROW** method of coaching. Let us explore what this is and
how to develop it.

GOALS IN THE CONTEXT OF GROW

The first step of the **GROW** model is the key step in the process.
Setting the goal gives you and your employee direction and
purpose. You will find it very difficult if you were handed a
bunch of tools and materials and told to build something
without a clear vision or goal of what is to be built.

The same holds true for developmental goals. It is not good enough to tell your employee they must improve in sales or build widgets faster. These types of goals create more confusion because they do not know where to start. Back to the building analogy, you may end up building a stool when what was really needed was a birdhouse. Clear goals are the cornerstone of the **GROW** model.

Here are some benefits to establishing goals upfront in the process:

- Both you and your employee have a better chance of starting in the right direction together.
- Coaching time is more efficient once goals are discussed upfront.
- You are able to plan ahead of the session and prepare targeted questions.
- The coaching session is direct and avoids meandering.
- You will come across more clear, instilling confidence in your employees.

Now, since we established the importance and benefit of goal setting early in the coaching process, let us look at identifying appropriate goal areas.

IDENTIFYING APPROPRIATE GOAL AREAS

When coaching, it is a temptation for you to talk more because we have plenty to say. However, in order to gain information and identifying appropriate goal areas, you must listen more. Remember, you have two ears and one mouth. Listen twice as much as you talk. Your objective here is to "catch" as much information as possible to help you determine what specific areas you can leverage and achieve results. Many times, allowing your employee to achieve even the smallest of goals begins a positive reinforcement of coaching. At some point before your actual coaching session, you want to engage in a brief discussion with your employee to determine their personal goals.

Here are some questions you should ask during your pre-coaching meeting. Remember to write down their answers for your reference later:

- What goals are you working on right now?
- Where are you in relation to those goals?
- What do you think is keeping you from reaching this goal?
- How will you know you reached that goal?

Asking these open-ended questions starts a conversation about your employee, which is what you want to achieve. Allowing your employee to speak more enables you to gather more information. Asking questions about their goals reveals their desires and this is something you can tie in to your coaching goal. Maybe an employee is furthering their education by going to college at night. Understanding this, you may be able to motivate your employee to achieve better performance, leading them to make more incentive they can use to fund their educational needs.

Furthermore, understanding where they are in relation to their goals reveals needs that may need support from you. Helping your employee with their personal goals builds a great working relationship. Finally, determining what roadblocks are preventing them from reaching their goals will provide insight into their personal circumstances. Granted, you may not solve all of your employee's problems, but demonstrating empathy goes a long way and helps to form goals for you that take into consideration your employee's personal situation. Remember, your employee does not care how much you know until you show how much you care. Listen more and talk less.

One final note, at first you may find asking questions challenging. This is normal. Give it time and do not give up. You may even have to let your employee know that you are interested more in their personal goals as a way to help them reach goals at work.

SETTING SMART GOALS

Writing goals can be a daunting task if done without a particular format or process. After you have your pre-coaching meeting with your employee, you are ready to meet again with your employee and write a clear goal, starting the GROW process. Having a clear format and goal development process will enable you build an effective goal. SMART is the technique you want to use when building the goal with your employee. It outlines your goal in an easy and clear format that your employee will find useful.

SMART stands for the following goal characteristics:

- **Specific**: What needs to be done? The goal must be clear. It cannot be a general statement like "be better at sales" or "be more organized". Use action verbs like increase sales or use a calendar. Next, we need to put some measurement in place.

- **Measurable**: Place some form of measurement that is easily verifiable to the goal. For example, continuing with the last example, increase sales by 3 percent or use a calendar two times a week. When you have a number incorporated to the goal, it makes it easier to check progress and hold your employee accountable.

- **Attainable**: Make sure the goal is not too much at one time to complete. Setting huge goals will lead to failure because the employee will see it as impossible. In addition, assess your employee's attitude. Use the information gained from your questions to help make this goal relevant. Irrelevant goals are not done. Make the goal manageable yet challenging.

- **Realistic**: Take in to consideration any learning, mentoring that has to take place or habits that have to be broken first before you set your employee's goal. If you are asking your employee to do something better, make sure they have the basics down first. Assess them, determine any gaps, and set your goals according to their skills and abilities.

- **Timely**: Always set a time limit or timeframe. Do not allow your employee's goal to wander aimlessly. Set follow up meetings and keep them. Your employee looks forward to these meetings especially when they are moving towards the goal. Do not set too much time between intervals. This may send the message to your employee that they have time to make the adjustment. You want to set short specific timeframes.

SMART goals are easy to do, but require a commitment on your part to use it consistently. Now that you have an idea how to develop your goal, we are going to see why understanding the reality is essential to the coaching process.

PRACTICAL ILLUSTRATION

Cory worked in the customer service department of the company he worked for. He had no defined goals except to help the customers with whatever problems they may have. Alex, the manager, approached Cory and asked for his satisfaction rating and other statistics relating to his work performance. While Cory worked hard, he had not been made aware that he needed to keep up with those statistics. Alex explained the process and set forth the goals that Cory would be expected to both reach and track. After that, Cory always had his performance reports ready and knew he was doing well.

Chapter Three:
Understanding the Realities

*Reality is that which, when you stop believing in it,
doesn't go away.*
Philip K. Dick

In the last chapter, you plotted a marker in the horizon as a beacon, guiding your employee to a specific, measurable, attainable, realistic, and timely goal. This is a great start, but there is also a need to know where your journey began. Placing a marker at the starting point of your employee's coaching journey enables both you and your employee to determine and measure progress. The goal in the offing may never seem to get any closer, because you have no point of reference to gauge your progress.

In this chapter, you will learn how to place that stake in the ground, marking the beginning of the coaching journey. Examining the current **realities** is the second component or the "R" of the GROW model. Let us delve into this concept to learn more about it.

GETTING A PICTURE OF WHERE YOU ARE

Framing the reality of the situation for your employee is an important step to accepting the coaching process. It is easier for you to outline your employee's performance problem, but this does not create the most receptive environment. In order to gain acceptance of the problem it is best to let the employees come to the realization themselves. Neglecting to do this could result in a non-responsive employee. They may feel apprehensive or defensive and shut down. They may go along with your coaching, but their attitude is that of just getting the coaching session over with in the least amount of time. Involving your employee is easy if you are willing to ask questions, listen, and guide your employee to where they are in their performance. Here are four simple questions you can ask:

- What is happening now?
- How often is this happening?
- When does it happen?
- What is the affect?

These questions help you to guide your employee to a place where they can see their performance affect the organization. When they realize the impact on their own more buy-in is created. In addition, more information may be obtained on why your employee is not performing at the level they should be achieving.

The realization of the problem marks the starting point. It also serves as a marker on performance. For instance, an employee may discover that they are not reaching production goals because they are taking extra time doing something incorrectly. Knowing this, you are able to refer to this issue when improvements occur.

IDENTIFYING OBSTACLES

When coaching, obstacles will arise and you need to be prepared to handle them with efficiency. The last thing you want to happen is your employee handing you an obstacle you cannot address because you are not prepared to handle the problem with a consistent response.

Using the IRA steps to obstacle identification and removal is vital to the coaching process. Here is the breakdown of the process.

- **Identify the obstacle**: Have a frank discussion with your employee and determine what is blocking their performance. Waiting for them to give you the information voluntarily will probably not happen.

- **Root out the cause**: Many times underlying emotions or problems may be the cause of the obstacles. Ask probing questions and jot down answers. You might realize they have a fear that must be addressed.

- **Antidote given**: A remedy to the situation is needed in order to get past this obstacle. Brainstorm with your employee on ways to remove the obstacles. In some cases, you may have to try several different antidotes. Be patient if the cause is genuine.

No matter what the perceived obstacles are, do not let it stifle your coaching objective. Rarely, you may encounter an employee that throws obstacles constantly your way in an effort to derail you. Identify this and address it with that employee, documenting every conversation.

EXPLORING THE PAST

Exploring your employees past performance and development is a great way to develop the reality of today's performance. Of course, you want to avoid belabouring a past mistake to the point where it makes the session ineffective. On the other hand, focusing on previous achievements helps to encourage your employee.

Here are some things to focus on from the past:

- Goals that were met
- Great behaviors
- Great attitudes
- Problems solved

Using the past helps to recap where your employee is at today. It is like telling a story but the end has not yet been determined. Use this time to speak positively to your employee. Avoid being negative or emphasizing the consequences to failure. This will leave an impression on your employee that could hinder their success.

Setting a positive environment opens the door for the next part of the GROW model. Developing options is an essential step both you and your employee must take in order to continue toward meeting your development goals. Let us explore what this entails.

PRACTICAL ILLUSTRATION

Gary worked as a receptionist. He had been told that he needed improvement by his supervisor Jenna, but not on what he needed to improve specifically. After a while, he was assigned a coach named Dan. Dan helped Gary map out what his current situation was, and then they set goals for improvement in the areas Gary might be lacking in. After a while, Gary felt a little better about his work, though he wasn't sure if he was really improving. Dan came back to assess Gary after the goals were set. When he compared the results to his original assessment, Gary was happy to find that he had improved as he had thought, and he had Dan to thank for that reassurance.

Chapter Four:
Developing Options

When a person acts without knowledge of what he thinks, feels,
needs, or wants, he does not yet have the option
of choosing to act differently.
Clarke Moustakas

This chapter discusses how to explore **options** that will enable your employee to move towards the goal that was set before them. This is the next component or the "O" in the GROW model. This is the pivotal step in the coaching process. If done correctly, you will engage your employee and create a desire for them to improve. If done incorrectly, your employee will disengage and they probably will fail again. It is the coach's job to create this participative environment. Let us look and see how.

IDENTIFYING PATHS

Many times, we feel that we have to outline the specific actions an employee has to take in order to reach the stated goal. While this may make you feel better, the likely hood of this action becoming meaningful to your employee is close to nil. Let us quickly review what we have done so far. You established what the goal is. There is usually very little wiggle room when it comes to a performance goal. It is the plain, unchangeable business reality. Next, we established the current state of affairs with respect to your employee's performance. This historical and factual reality is also unchangeable.

Now, let us take it from the employee's perspective. How in control do they feel? Would they shut down if we, as their coach, solely determine the action steps they are going to take? They might. It is imperative to keep the employee engaged. If not, the rest of the coaching session is just a one-way discussion, leaving your employee powerless in his or her own development.

When you allow your employee to participate in the development of their options, you get B.I.G. results. B.I.G. results stand for the following benefits:

- **Buy-in** by your employee, because the options developed was a collaborative effort

- **Innovation**, because more creativity is possible when two work at it

- **Growth**, because the options developed will have more meaning and lasting commitment

CHOOSING YOUR FINAL APPROACH

Deciding on which option to implement could be frustrating. The best thing to do is to implement a consistent method to determining the best possible option. The APAC section of the B.I.G. template is designed to help you come to a quick decision on which option to implement. Here is how it works.

After you have brainstormed your options with your employee, assess the pros of each option. Determine the benefits and possible rewards to selection that option. Write those benefits in the template. Next, assess the cons for each option. Here are some things to consider:

- Resources needed
- Cost
- Time
- Return on investment
- Disruption of the business

All of these factors could rule out an option. Once you identify the cons, place those in the corresponding area on the template. Next, determine the top five options that are feasibility to implement. Use a rating scale from 1-5 and place that in the rating column. Now, you are ready to rate the relevancy of the options identified as feasible. Rate the relevancy of the options to the goal. Here are some things to consider when rating this category:

- Does this option build new supporting skills?
- Does this option meet the time requirement of the goal?
- Is this option measurable?

Once you determine the relevancy, you are able to multiply the feasibility rating with the relevancy rating. The highest number is possibly your best option. Remember to gain consensus from your employee on this option.

STRUCTURING A PLAN

Since you have your employee's attention, it is best to begin the planning process. Structuring a plan as soon as possible sends the message to your employee you mean business when it comes to implementing the option. For example: your SMART goal may be to increase the sales attempt rate from five percent to seven in 30 days. Next, you and your employee may have agreed to focus on asking open-ended questions during a sales call as their option, giving them more information to help them attempt better. When are they going to start asking those questions? How many are they going to ask? These are action items you want to document in a preliminary plan.

The **3T** questioning technique helps you document three major milestones. Basically, you ask, "What are you going to do":

- Tomorrow?
- Two weeks from today?
- Thirty days from today?

You may need to guide your employee when answering the first question. Remember the more time you let pass from the time you coach them and the time you implement your first action step, you could be losing precious information discussed in your coaching session.

Here is an example of how the earlier scenario could be developed:

Coach: "You said you wanted to ask more open-ended questions to help you attempt better sales. Great, what steps are you going to take tomorrow to begin that process? "

Employee: "I can try asking an open ended question on every few calls."

Coach: "Do you think you can ask a question on every third call?"

Employee: "Okay, I will try to ask on every third call."

Coach: "Let's look ahead two weeks from now. Do you think you can increase the frequency to every other call?"

Employee: "That sounds fair."

Coach: "Great, now, let's shoot to ask questions on every call 30 days from now. What do you think?"

Employee: "I believe I can do this or get really close."

Coach: "Let's write this down on paper and put a final plan together."

Once you get to this point, you are ready to begin drafting your final plan. Let us see what this involves.

PRACTICAL ILLUSTRATION

Darren was assigned to help Perry by coaching him. Perry didn't have a big enough budget for marketing. Darren decided it would be best to hear Perry and his ideas on options to solving the issue. After they both collaborated and pulled together some viable options, they had to make a decision. They compared the costs in both time and resources of each option, while also taking the potential return on the investments into consideration. They eventually came to the decision to focus the marketing strategy on a central medium rather than spread it out more thinly. The marketing venture was a success, and it was because of the collaboration of the two of them.

Chapter Five:
Wrapping it All Up

A good plan today is better than a perfect plan tomorrow.
Chinese Proverb

In the last chapter, your goal was to get your employee participating in the coaching process by identifying action steps together. It is time now to solidify what has been said and established as actions steps or simply stated—wrapping it all up.

In this chapter, you are going to learn how to finalize your employee's plan in a way that motivates them to take action immediately. Wrapping up the coaching session is the final component or the "W" in the GROW model to coaching. This step is crucial, because it should set things in motion quickly, which is your goal. Let us see how.

CREATING THE FINAL PLAN

When creating a development plan, there must be consistent steps outlined, allowing your employee the opportunity to learn, apply measure, and assess their development. The LAMA process is designed to approach the planning activity in a consistent and efficient manner.

Each component of the LAMA process is time sensitive and is anchored by your overall SMART goal, meaning the entire process should be complete by the goal day you set. Here is the breakdown of LAMA and a description of each of the components:

- **Learn**: some form of learning should take place. It could be a variety of activities. Mentoring with a peer, reading a book, taking a course, are some examples of learning opportunities you may implement.

- **Apply**: implement what was learnt soon after learning is completed.

- **Measure**: agree on a method of measuring when and how the new learning is used on the job. You can perform observations, or have your employee track it on a worksheet you developed. The idea is to monitor the use of the new knowledge.

- **Assess**: review the impact of the new skill on the performance metric being improved. Any success should be attributed to the new skill and encouraged.

As mentioned earlier, each component must have a start and an end date. The assessment date should correspond to the SMART goal date. If your SMART goal timeframe is greater than 30 days, you should plan more assessment dates and coach according to the performance results.

Since you now have a basic idea how to create that final plan, let us look at how to determine the first step.

IDENTIFYING THE FIRST STEP

The first step to any development activity is to learn. Allowing the employees to learn something new is essential to their overall development. There are many benefits to making learning a deliberate practice in a coaching process.

Here is a summary of benefits:

- Employee feels valued with the investment you are making in them

- You demonstrate that you care which helps to foster a better working relationship

- You give a chance for a role model to become a mentor to your employee

- New skills learned could be shared with other employees

Now you understand some of the benefits to learning. Let us look at ways you are able to motivate your employee.

GETTING MOTIVATED

Motivating your employee is an essential part of coaching. Many times, motivating by money alone is not enough. Employees prefer to have a great working environment and a good relationship with their manager. It is the manager's job to create this environment. Here is a helpful way to create the supportive and motivating environment your employees need to thrive.

The process is called the five B's now this process requires you to re-think the way you manage. If you find yourself challenged by this topic, seek out additional resources that will help you develop the skills and behaviors necessary to foster a motivating atmosphere.

The five B's are the following:

- Be consistent in your coaching. Coach all of your employees. Do not reserve coaching for only your "problem "employees.

- Be respectful with your employees. Being a manager does not give you the ability to insult or berate your employees.

- Be caring and watch your employees' behavior for signs of personal issues. The goal is to guide them when they are experiencing problems both in and outside of work. Of course, you are not going to get personally involved, but you want to lend an empathetic ear and guide them to resources that may help them.

- Be flexible and find ways to reward you employees with non-monetary items. Perhaps some time off away from their desk doing something else or cross training is a possibility.

- Be a cheerleader and celebrate even the smallest of successes. Give recognition the way your employees prefer. Some may like public recognition while others prefer low-key ones. Find out what your employees prefer and use it strategically.

Taking the time to motivate your employees is a worthwhile investment. Make sure you plan it and implement it without fail or else your coaching efforts will be in vain. Next, let us look at the importance of trust in the coaching environment.

PRACTICAL ILLUSTRATION

Aaron was an office worker for a paper sales company. He had been nearly stagnant until his coach Windy came along. After the identification of the problem and a collaborated plan of action, Aaron was nearly ready. Wendy first made sure he had learned to better organize, and then she finalized the plan with a call to action. Aaron had specific goals and deadlines he needed to adhere to, so he began working to meet those goals immediately. After a follow up assessment, Wendy determined that Aaron had shown substantial improvement, and made sure to congratulate him.

Chapter Six:
The Importance of Trust

Without trust, words become the hollow sound of a wooden gong. With trust, words become life itself.
Anonymous

In your coaching session with your employees, you will discover many times things about your employee that are personal and sensitive topics. This is normal and demonstrates trust in you. As their coach, establishing and maintaining trust is the most essential ingredient to the entire process. If your employee determines that your purpose of improving their performance is to further your career, then they will not trust you. Without trust, whatever you say and do will be subject to skepticism.

This chapter discusses the meaning of trust, its relationship to coaching and building trust. Building trust must be a sincere desire in you. It requires an investment in time and emotion. Anything less will not foster a trusting relationship between you and your employee. First, let us begin by defining what trust is.

WHAT IS TRUST?

In the next couple of lessons, we are going to discuss trust. Coaching should be a place where you and your employee can discuss things openly. Having a trusting relationship with your employees is essential to the coaching process. Without trust, you will seldom get to the root cause of issues that could be hindering their performance.

Trust is built over time and is accomplished through your actions. Trust, in the realm of coaching, could be defined as the ability to instill confidence, and reliance in you by being fair, truthful, honorable, and competent in what you do as a manager. Lacking in any of these areas could hinder you instilling trust into your employees.

Let us look at how trust works in coaching.

TRUST AND COACHING

Effective coaching is done in a trusting environment. There is no doubt about this. In order for you to be able to inspire your employees to perform better, they have to trust you. Your coaching session is the only opportunity to demonstrate to them that they can trust you because you use the coaching session as a tool for building up employees and not tearing them down.

Avoid using your coach session as a venue to deliver reprimands, sanctions, bad news, etc. This is not the place for that kind of information. In addition, avoid using coaching when only negative things need to be addressed. Coaching should be a purposeful event that happens regularly and is void of negative information. This is not to say you cannot discuss performance issues. It just has to be presented in a way that speaks of development than of punishment.

When coaching, we should avoid being a DOPE, or

- **Degrading** your employees

    o Using negative words like stupid, lazy, slacker, etc.

- **Ostracizing** your employee

    o Using coaching sessions only as a means for disciplinary action

- **Punishing** your employee

    o Using sessions to deliver sanctions or firing them

- **Evaluating** your employee

    o Telling employees that they are the worst performer,

    o Why can't they be like the other good employees, etc.

Make coaching a haven for encouragement and development and not a place for stress and discouragement. Without trust, you will not be able to coach well. Next, let us look at how to build trust.

BUILDING TRUST

Building trust takes practice and dedication to being sensitive to your employee's needs. Here are eight steps to building trust with your employees in and out of the coaching session:

1. Maintain positive body language

2. Listen to them intently and speak less

3. Always respect your employees

4. Keep things confidential

5. Keep your promises

6. Be honest and transparent

7. Be confident

8. Tell them you believe in them

Next, let us learn ways to provide feedback in a positive yet serious manner.

PRACTICAL ILLUSTRATION

Ringo was an active sales coach for the company, and knew how to gain and keep the trust of other employees. He knew that without it, the entire coaching process would be compromised. He never spoke harshly or negatively to the employee he was coaching, and was always completely honest with them. He found that the more he respected and trusted the employee, the more the employee respected and trusted him. This genuine attitude helped make Ringo a more effective and helpful coach to the employees and made them better employees as well.

Chapter Seven:
Providing Feedback

*I've learned that mistakes can often be as good a
teacher as success.*
Jack Welch

In the last chapter, we discussed the importance of establishing trust and its relation to the coaching process. Although building trust is a personal investment you must make, you are still required to provide both negative and positive feedback.

Understanding how to structure feedback is essential in balancing trust with the need to discuss desired and undesired behaviors with your employee. In this chapter, you are going to learn techniques for delivering feedback well.

THE FEEDBACK SANDWICH

Initiating the feedback process could be a stressful situation if done incorrectly. However, as managers, we have to make tough discussions with our employees. In the world of giving feedback, time is of the essence. You want to be comfortable when giving feedback. When you are comfortable, your employee will be comfortable.

The Feedback Sandwich is a method of introducing feedback to your employee surrounded by praise. It starts the conversation by briefly reviewing a positive aspect your employee is currently demonstrating. It could be a good attitude; a well-executed sales pitch, etc. Be careful not to spend too much time praising at the beginning, because the "meat" of your feedback message will be diluted. Remember, the reason why you are speaking to your employee at this time is to deliver feedback.

Next, deliver the opportunity for growth in a positive tone. Avoid accusing your employee, but remain focused on the message you must deliver. In the next lesson, we will discuss how to structure constructive criticism. For now, remember this is the largest part of your dialogue.

Finally, close the feedback session on a positive note. Praise the employee on a strength they have or tell them you are confident they are going to adjust and be successful. This helps the employee overcome the embarrassment that is associated with receiving feedback.

To review, you want to structure your feedback sandwich by starting with Praise, then delivering the opportunity for growth and closing with praise again. This is easy to remember if you recall the acronym **POP**.

Here is a sample delivery:

Praise: *John, your sales attempts this month are doing well because you are asking good probing questions up front and I appreciate your work.*

Opportunity for growth: *Here is something I noticed. When a customer says, "No" to your attempt, you immediately stop selling and abandon the sales attempt. This is where you should use more questions. As a result, your sales percentage is one of the lowest on the team.*

Praise: *I know you are capable of asking more questions because you build good rapport with our customers.*

PROVIDING CONSTRUCTIVE CRITICISM

Providing constructive criticism is a skill that requires you to focus on four key areas.

First, focus on one issue at a time. Avoid addressing multiple issues. This will only cause confusion and frustration. Identify the issue and set a plan on how you are going to address this.

Second, focus on being timely. Once you identify an issue, make sure you do not wait too long to deliver the critique. The more time passes the less affective it will be. Your employee may even forget what they did.

Third and most importantly, focus on observable actions or behaviors. Avoid generalities. For example, do not say, "You have an issue with time management." This statement is lacking an observable action or behavior. Instead, you might want to say, "I notice you spend extra time talking to other employees on your way to meetings, making you late to most of them." The observable behavior is "talking to other employees." With this behavior identified, you are now able to focus on the next point.

Fourth, focus on a plan to change the behaviour. Depending on the extent of change that must happen, your plan may be a simple adjustment. However, if it is complex, then use your SMART goal writing technique to help your employee set successful goals.

Now let us learn how to encourage growth and development.

ENCOURAGING GROWTH AND DEVELOPMENT

Encouraging growth and development is really providing opportunities to learn. When we give opportunities to our employees, we send the message that we value them and are willing to invest time, effort, and sometimes money into their development.

As managers, we should foster an environment of learning. Here are some ways you are able to provide learning opportunities for your employees:

- Develop a peer mentorship process

- Use your internal training department

- Second your employee to another department to learn something new

- Start a book of the month club where your employees read, on company time, a few pages at a time

- Use your team meeting as a venue for team learning

- Send your employees to seminars if your budget allows

A good approach is to create a menu of opportunities for your employees to learn. Remember that learning styles vary among adults. Therefore, try different approaches.

PRACTICAL ILLUSTRATION

Mary was a good coach, but she found it difficult to give feedback when an employee's work was less than expected or they didn't reach the goals that were set. Mary knew that when she needed to mention something for the employee to work on, it was often a good idea to let them know of the areas they have improved on or excel at. When constructive criticism has to be given, Mary remembers to always weigh the good with the bad to ensure that the employee understands their value and is more receptive to the negative aspects of the criticism.

Chapter Eight:
Overcoming Roadblocks

*Obstacles are those frightful things you see when
you take your eyes off your goal.*
Henry Ford

It is common to encounter roadblocks during the coaching process. Roadblocks manifest in many different forms. Roadblocks, however, should not spell an end to the coaching process. You should expect roadblocks to occur. It is natural for it to happen because we are expecting behavior change, which that in and of itself is a task for your employee.

In this chapter, we will discuss ways to overcoming roadblocks. Some of the things you will learn are identifying common roadblocks re-evaluate goals and focus on progress. Roadblocks are not dead ends. They are warning signs that will help you identify when you need to intervene and get your employee back on track.

COMMON OBSTACLES

Coaching takes two people to accomplish. The manager must be just as engaged as the employee. Lack of zeal and honesty creates roadblocks that will hinder your employee's ability to reach their goals. Here are some common obstacles we as managers create:

- Do not have enough time to coach properly
- Lack of confidence in coaching

- Fear of confrontation
- Feeling awkward
- Fear of failure in coaching
- Afraid employee will not respond

Now, from the employee's perspective, here are some common obstacles they may encounter:

- Home/life issues are blocking progress
- Fear of losing their job
- Lack of confidence reaching the goal
- Denial there is anything wrong
- Poor relationship with the coach

Obstacles come in many different forms. However, the root of the obstacles typically comes from a personal deficiency in their life situation. Maslow's theory of needs outlines basic needs we all must have in order to reach higher needs. Here is brief overview of the needs.

- Physical need
- Safety need
- Social need
- Esteem need
- Growth need

The basics of all needs are the physical and safety needs. If a person is lacking in either of these areas, they will find it difficult to progress further into the higher needs. For example, if you know your employee is having issues at home, their physical or safety need may be at risk, creating an obstacle to reaching a goal, which is a higher order need. When faced with a needs issue, try your best to acknowledge the need and guide them to a qualified resource to assist them with this issue.

Let us look at how to re-evaluate goals and realign the employee back to achieving the goal.

RE-EVALUATING GOALS

As time passes from the original coaching session, you want to check in on your employee and see where they are at, in respect to the goal that was set. It is at this point, where you may want to re-evaluate the goal and determine if it is still SMART.

There are several things you want to take into consideration when re-evaluating goals. First, re-evaluating does not mean that you have to change it. Re-evaluating is an opportunity to check on the goal and to determine how your employee is doing in achieving this goal. Here are some steps you want to take when re-evaluating a goal:

- Revisit the starting point. You want to review where you began. This way you are able to see if progress has been made and your employee is moving towards the goal.

- Determine what has been accomplished. Look at what the current performance level is and compare it to the starting point determined earlier.

- Review the amount of time left in respect to the goal date. You want to see if the amount of improvement is aligned with how much time has passed or how much time is left before the goal date is reached.

- Determine if the time remaining before the goal date is adequate to fulfill the goal. Here you want to see if there is still enough time to improve and reach the goal.

- If not enough time is left to accomplish goal by goal date, then set a new goal and goal date based on how much improvement has been accomplished and the time it took to get there.

- If there is still enough time, set smaller goals to help the employee move towards the established general goal.

In overcoming roadblocks, you may need to be more flexible. Perhaps the goal originally seemed like a viable goal, but when put into practice it becomes apparent that you will not be able to reach it. Do not become frustrated. Be flexible and understanding of your employee if you have to reset a goal.

FOCUSING ON PROGRESS

If you find yourself with an employee struggling with reaching their goals, you may be tempted to pull them over and discuss how they are missing the mark and the related consequences.

Focusing on the negative aspects will only create more obstacles. Remember the hierarchy of needs mentioned earlier? Well, if you start making the coaching session feel more negative, the employee may feel that their job is threatened. If this happens, they will become more fearful and this adds to the roadblocks.

Instead of focusing on the negatives, focus on the progress. Tell your employee that you see progress and that you believe that they are able to make their goals. Speaking positively expands the employee's belief about themselves. Use encouraging phrases like the ones here:

- I know you are not quite there yet, but you managed to improve this much in such a short amount of time.

- Your progress is steady and you are showing promise that you will reach that goal.

- You showed definite improvement since our last discussion. I am confident you are going to hit this goal.

It is easy to speak into the positive aspects of progress. The benefits of focusing on progress could reap the following:

- Increased communication between you and your employee

- Build trust

- Increase motivation

- Goal is reached

- Build good relationship with your employee

- Employee's confidence is boosted

You see if you speak positively, then positive things come out, but if you speak negatively, and then you will get a negative reaction.

PRACTICAL ILLUSTRATION

Bob knew that as a coach, he and the employee he works with may face obstacles. Upon first meeting Rory, Bob had feelings of doubt in his ability to coach him. Regardless, Bob continued without a hitch. Rory and Bob developed a good relationship. Bob eventually had to re-evaluate the goals that he and Rory had originally made. He found that while Rory was making progress, he was not making the progress in a timely fashion. After a few adjustments to their original options, they came to a solution that continued Rory's progress and allowed him to reach his goal in time. Bob also gained confidence in himself as a coach.

Chapter Nine:
Reaching the End

The reason goals are not reached is that we spend time
doing second things first.
Robert J. McKain

Identifying the end of the coaching process for a particular goal is a vital step that helps both you and your employee acknowledge you have both reached the end. Failing to acknowledge the achievement of a goal could result in disappointment for your employee. Many times, they are anticipating the end and perhaps expect some form of celebration or kudos. No matter how you do it, as a coach, you must know when your employee has reached their goal and acknowledge it.

In this chapter, you will learn to recognize success, transition your employee from this coaching goal to another and wrapping it up. Let us begin by discussing how to know when you have achieved success.

How to Know When You've Achieved Success

Determining if success is achieved is a crucial element to the coaching process. If you fail to recognize success, you could hurt your coaching programme. Your employee worked hard to reach their goals and it is your job to recognize when it has been achieved.

Taking stock of your employee's accomplishments helps you to determine how well your employee has achieved success. This stock taking could also help you determine if your employee is ready to move into the next level of their development.

Here are some areas to review when taking inventory:

- Review the goals and compare them to how well your employee achieved them

- Review where your employee is at the beginning of the coaching process and how far they have progressed

- List the behaviors your employee demonstrated during the coaching progress

- List your employee's strengths

- List your employee's weaknesses

- List your expectations and compare them to how well your employee meets or exceeds your expectations

- If applicable, determine if your employee is ready for the next level of their development

If you noticed, there are two levels of success. The first level deals with the immediate goal. During the course of developing your employee, you probably set various goals. You may use this list to determine if they are successful in one goal and then move on to the next goal.

On the other hand, you may use this to help you determine if your employee has achieved overall success and is ready to move on to more development in other areas like management.

TRANSITIONING THE COACHEE

Transitioning is moving your employee to the next level of development. You may also transition your employee to the next developmental goal. In any case, it is a good practice to make a clear transition. Making it clear tells the employee they achieved success and are ready to take on new challenges.

Failure to transition may frustrate the employee over time. Transitioning closes a door and opens the next. Below are the steps to making a good transition:

- Make a statement of success. This is a purposeful announcement you make to your employee as a way to mark the transition. Here is a sample:

"John, you have accomplished a great deal over the last year. Today marks the beginning of a new phase of development for you."

- Overview of accomplishments given: here you review what your employee has accomplished and how well they did and that you are proud of them

- Verify your employee agrees. You want to ensure that you and your employee are on the same page. They may not quickly understand that you are about to move them into another level of development. Use open-ended questions to help you determine if your employee is in fact ready to transition. If they are not ready, then set goals to help them address those concerns and coach them through it, using SMART goals and the GROW coaching process.

- Engage the employee with the next level of development. You should have a plan in place that outlines the transition. Share this plan with your employee and have them engage it as soon as possible. Perhaps you may have to hand them off to another manager for development, then walk the employee over to that manager and introduce them.

If your purpose is to transition your employee to the next development goal, then follow the steps like before and create the new goal. Always make sure your employee is ready for the next level of development.

WRAPPING IT ALL UP

Wrapping it all up is just a matter of organizing your employee's coaching file and transitioning the file to the next manager for reference. Even if you do not plan to transition your employee over to a new manager, wrap up the coaching file and keep it accessible for future use.

Here are some things you want to do so you can wrap this coaching file up:

- Have all your coaching documents related to your employee placed in a file folder. If it is electronic, do the same.

- Use a wrap up worksheet and place that as the first page of the coaching file. A "wrapping it up" worksheet should outline the following:

  - Employee's profile (i.e. name, years at organization, job title, etc.)

  - List of achievements

  - List of positive behaviors

  - List of areas for further development

  - List of goals your employee would like to achieve

  - Your overall assessment

  - Your recommendation

  - Brief outline of the next events

Your employee's coaching sessions are now transitioning into something else. Let us look at what mentoring is and how to leverage that as a form of development for your employee.

PRACTICAL ILLUSTRATION

Rob coached John on his sales performance. Rob determined that John had completed his goal in the six-month period they had agreed upon and was ready to start transitioning towards a new goal. Rob congratulated John on his vast improvement since the start of the coaching, and made sure John was ready for the transition. Rob was satisfied and made a positive recommendation when he turned in his overall report on John's progress. John had exceeded expectations and was ready for the next stage of development. Rob had improved as well in his experience and confidence in his own coaching abilities.

Chapter Ten:
How Mentoring Differs from Coaching

Mentoring is a brain to pick, an ear to listen,
and a push in the right direction.
John Crosby

Earlier we defined the terms coaching and mentoring. We learned that both concepts vary greatly in terms of the goal each sought to achieve. In this chapter, you are going to learn the practical differences and blend the two for a balanced development program. In addition, we will discover how to integrate the GROW model when you are mentoring your employee and finally, you will learn how to focus more on building relationships. Let us start by comparing the practical differences between coaching and mentoring.

THE BASIC DIFFERENCES

There are differences between coaching and mentoring. Each typically has goals to accomplish, but the methods are vastly different.

Coaching has the following characteristics:

- Interaction is usually not voluntary

- The interaction usually is for a set amount of time.

- The interaction is structured and meetings are typically confined to scheduled meetings

- Coach does not necessarily have to be an expert on the coaching topic

- Generally, the interaction is short-termed and focus is usually in one or two areas of development

- The focus is on a particular job function developmental issue

- The goal is to produce a more immediate change or result

- Coaching is typically targeting specific opportunities for improvement

Mentoring has the following characteristics:

- Interaction is usually voluntary

- Relationship is usually long-term over an extensive period of time

- Interaction is less structured with more causal than structured meetings

- Mentor is usually regarded as an expert in their field and is a resource to the protégé

- Career development is the overall goal of mentoring

- The goal is to develop areas that the protégé deems necessary for their development for future roles

- Mentoring targets the entire career path of a protégé

Let us see how we can blend the two models for an effective development program for your employees.

BLENDING THE TWO MODELS

Depending on the type of working environment you have and the overall goal of your employee, you may want to combine the characteristics of coaching with mentorship. What you decide to use depends on the current work environment, the type of advancement opportunity your employee has and the time you or someone else have to give to develop the target employee.

There is no right or wrong answer when determining which characteristic you want to combine. Simply pick the ones that will help you achieve maximum results. For example, you may want to blend the more casual approach to meeting with your employee with a targeted area of development. On the other hand, you may want to blend the relationship-building aspect of mentoring to the planned meeting intervals.

The approach you determine is considered the best for your environment. Here is a list of benefits you realize when you combine coaching with mentorship:

- Increased flexibility

- Allows you to supervise your employee while acting autonomous

- Allows your employee to determine what they want to develop

- Your employee will feel more empowered in their development

- You can enlist the help of other managers in the development of your employee

- Greater satisfaction for both you and your employee

In essence, blending the two models provides more flexibility with the monitoring you need to ensure your employee is on the path to career development.

ADAPTING THE GROW MODEL FOR MENTORING

Adapting the GROW model to mentoring is very easy to do. When coaching, the GROW model is used as a guide for the coach to structure their dialogue with their employee. The coach develops the goal and guides the employee to reach a goal the coach selects.

In mentoring, the GROW model is used as a guide to questioning the protégé on what development path they want seek. Here the mentor asks open-ended questions that form the basis of the mentoring program. Here are some questions you can use when you want to use GROW for mentoring purposes:

- **Goal**: What are your career goals? What do you want to accomplish in the next year?

- **Reality**: Where are you in relation to your career goal? What are you lacking that you need to have in order to reach that career goal?

- **Options**: What activities do you think will help you develop those missing skills? How do you want to go about developing the skills necessary to advance your career?

- **Wrap it up**: What is your plan? How do you want to go about this?

FOCUSING ON THE RELATIONSHIP

When you coach, the relationship is hierarchal, meaning that you are driving the process and the employee must respond. Mentoring is not meant to be set up that way. Mentoring is a shoulder-to-shoulder type relationship. In coaching your focus is on reaching goals with a targeted development plan.

On the other hand, mentoring is sharing and guiding your protégé. It requires less structure but more relationship building. Being a mentor to someone creates a special relationship where the mentor watches over the protégé, guides them, and corrects them in different situations. There is not a set intervention. It is constant awareness, looking out for pitfalls and political traps that are common in the work environment.

Mentors also become more involved in the protégé's life, demonstrating caring, understanding, and guiding them through it from the employment perspective. Deep personal issues should be taken care of by professionals; however, guiding them to that professional level is a mentor's job.

Here are some behaviors that help to foster a good relationship between a mentor and a protégé:

- Demonstrate caring by listening for issues that are not readily disclosed to you. Perhaps you over hear a conversation where your protégé is struggling with something. Demonstrate care by encouraging your protégé to discuss it with you.

- Demonstrate understanding by acknowledging and empathizing with your employees situation. Take the time to fully grasp what is going on and acknowledge it is real and that you would feel the same if you were in their shoes.

- Demonstrate listening by giving your undivided attention and avoid interruptions when talking with them like answering the telephone or looking at email. Notate and mirror things back to your protégé to demonstrate you are listening.

- Demonstrate respect by keeping the relationship professional at all times. Avoid degrading your protégé or using causal language in front of others. Show you respect your employee as if they were an equal.

Keeping an eye on the relationship is just as important as keeping focus on the goal. The mentor-protégé relationship is delicate because the employee must see the value of the relationship. If they do not see a relationship, then the purpose for mentoring is gone.

PRACTICAL ILLUSTRATION

Dave was the floor manager of a paper mill. He was asked to coach a sales representative named Jerry so that he may more effectively help the company. Dave wanted to devote more time to Jerry, but was still needed as the floor manager. Dave decided upon a blend of coaching and mentoring so that he could still remain the floor manager and coach Jerry at the same time. The combination of the two methods did more than that though. He soon realized that Jerry was benefiting as well. He had a sense of empowerment and confidence because he was more influential in his development, and he was receiving coaching from a variety of experienced managers and supervisors that gave him a bigger source of knowledge to draw from. Dave felt the compromise worked out for both of them.

- **Lee Iacocca**: I have found that being honest is the best technique I can use. Right up front, tell people what you're trying to accomplish, and what you're willing to sacrifice to accomplish it.

- **John Wooden**: If you're not making mistakes, then you're not doing anything. I'm positive that a doer makes mistakes.

- **Pearl Buck**: I don't wait for moods. You accomplish nothing if you do that. Your mind must know it has got to get down to earth.

- **Warren Buffett**: I don't look to jump over 7-foot bars. I look around for 1-foot bars that I can step over.

- **George Allen**: People of mediocre ability sometimes achieve outstanding success because they don't know when to quit. Most men succeed because they are determined to.

- **George Halas**: What makes a good coach? Complete dedication.

www.ingramcontent.com/pod-product-compliance
Lightning Source LLC
Chambersburg PA
CBHW070931180526
45168CB00003B/1023

* 9 7 8 1 5 1 7 3 6 7 2 8 2 *